Introduction

The unique characteristics of animals is a miscellany of facts, genuine or supposed, gleamed from earlier and contemporary Greek writers (No Latin writer is once named) and to a limited extent from his own observation to illustrate the habits of the animal world.

We are of course prepared to encounter much that modern science rejects, but the general tone with its search after the picturesque, the startling, even the miraculous, would justify us in ranking Aelian with the paradoxical, rather than with the sober exponents of natural history.

Mythology, mariners' yarns, vulgar superstitions, the ascertained facts of nature—all serve to adorn a tale and, on occasion, to point a moral. His religion is the popular stoicism of the age. Aleian repeatedly affirms his belief in the gods and in divine providence; the wisdom and beneficence of Nature are held up to veneration; the folly and selfishness of man are contrasted with the untaught virtues of the animal world. Some animals, to be sure, have their failings, but he chooses rather to dwell upon their good qualities, devotion, courage, self-sacrifice, gratitude. Again, animals are guided by reason, and from them we may learn contentment, control of the passions, and calm in the face of death.

His primary object is to entertain and while so doing to convey instruction in the most agreeable form. Some might find fault with his random and piece-meal handling of his theme-of which he is well aware, and he defends himself with the plea that a frequent change of topic helps to maintain the reader's interest and saves him from boredom.

As to the permanent value of his work he has no misgivings and since we have been informed that his writings were much admired, we may assume that they appealed to cultivated circles in a way that the voluminous and possibly arid compilations of grammarians did not.

Now I am well aware of the labour that others have expended on this subject, yet I have collected all the materials that I could; I have clothed them in untechnical language, and am persuaded that my achievement is a treasure far from negligible. So if anyone considers them profitable, let him make use of them; anyone who does not consider them so may give them to his father to keep and attend to.

Animal Peculiarity Volume 2 Part 5

By T.P Just

~~~

Animal Peculiarity Volume 1 [1-8]
Animal Peculiarity Volume 2 [1-8]
Just Enterprises

Table of Contents

2. The Hake

The Hake though not differing widely from other fish in its inward parts is nevertheless solitary in its habits and cannot endure to live with other fish.
It is the only fish that has its heart in its belly and stones in its brain resembling millstones. At the rising of the Dog-star it alone lurks in its den, while other fish are in the habit of doing so in the very frostiest seasons.

3. The Crab and Music

Those who hunt Crabs have hit upon the device of luring them with music. At any rate they catch them by means of a flageolet (this is the name of an instrument). Now the Crabs have gone down into their hiding-places, and the men begin to play.

And at the sound, as though by a spell, the Crabs are induced to quit their den, and then captivated with delight even emerge from the sea. But the flute players withdraw backwards and the Crabs follow and when on the dry lands are caught.

The Sprat and Music

Those who live by the lake of Marea catch the Sprats there by singing with the almost shrillness, accompanying their song with the clash of castanets.

And the fishes, like women dancing, leap to the tune and fall into the nets spread for their capture. And through their dancing and frolics the Egyptians obtain an abundant catch.

Egyptian magic

I am informed that the Egyptians bring birds down from the sky by some magic peculiar to them. And they have certain spells to bewitch snakes and draw them without any difficulty from their lurking places.

4. The Beaver

The Beaver is an amphibious creature: by day it lives hidden in rivers, but at night it roams the land, feeding itself with anything that it can find.

Now it understands the reason why hunters come after it with such eagerness and impetuosity, and it puts down its head and with its teeth cuts off its testicles and throws them in their path, as a prudent man who, falling into the hands of robbers, sacrifices all that he is carrying, to save his life, and forfeits his possessions by way of ransom.

If however it has already saved its life by self-castration and is again pursued, then it stands up and reveals that it offers no ground for their eager pursuit, and releases the hunters from all further exertions, for they esteem its flesh less.

Often however Beavers with testicles intact, after escaping as far away as possible, have drawn in the coveted part, and with great skill and ingenuity tricked their pursuers, pretending that they no longer possessed what they were keeping in concealment.

5. The Ichneumon

But I am told that the Ichneumon destroys the eggs of the Asp with intent to do away with the future enemies of its own young. And there is a story that the Libyan Asp even blinds men with its breath.

The Buprestids

The Buprestids (cow-inflator) is a creature which, if swallowed by a cow, causes it to swell and presently to burst and die.

The Caterpillar

Caterpillars feed upon vegetables and in a short, while destroy them. But they in turn are destroyed if a Woman with her monthly courses upon her walks through the vegetables.

The Gadfly

The worst enemies of cattle are the Gadfly and the Horsefly. The Gadfly is the size of the very largest flies, and its sting is powerful and long, and it makes a harsh buzzing sound.

The Horsefly

But the Horsefly is like the dog fly: its buzz is louder than the Gadfly, fly but its sting is smaller.

The Asp

Among all those who have been bitten by an Asp there is no record of a single man having escaped disaster. That is why (I am told) the Kings of Egypt Wear asps embroidered upon their crowns, hinting through the figure of the aforesaid creature at the invincibility of their rule.

Its bite fatal

There are Asps as much as five cubits long; the majority are black or of an ashy hue; and one may even see a red one. Those who have been bitten by an Asp do not live for more than four hours and are assailed by choking and convulsions and retching, so they say.

6. Animals abhor incest

Now does not Nature claim our admiration for this reason especially, besides others? Of the males. . The sires destroy most of the male fawns to prevent their multiplying and then mounting their dams.

Even among brute beasts, I fancy, such an act is regarded as bringing defilement and a curse. But Cyrus and Parasitic, you men of Persia, thought it a fine and legitimate action.

And Cyrus conceived a vile passion for his mother, a passion which his mother reciprocated. (While animals are moderate in their desires) men desire everything and stop at nothing.

7. Heracles revered by Mice

There is an island in the Black Sea named after Heracles which has been highly honored. Now all the Mice there pay reverence to the god, and every offering that is made to him they believe to have been made to gratify him and would not touch it.

And so the vine grows luxuriantly in his honor and is reverenced as an offering to him alone, while the ministers of the god preserve the clusters for their sacrifices. Accordingly when the grapes reach maturity the Mice quit the island so that they may not, by remaining, even involuntarily touch what is better not touched.

Later when the season has run its course they return to their own haunts. This is a merit in the Pontiac Mice. But Hippo, Diagrams, and Hero stratus, and all the rest in the tale of heaven's enemies, how would they have kept their hands off the grapes or other offerings-men who preferred by one means or another to rob the gods of their names and functions.

8. The Mouse in Egypt

This is what commonly happens in Egypt. When it rains in Egypt (the raindrops are minute) Mice are produced forthwith. Now they roam the plough lands and damage the standing crops by cutting away and nibbling the ears of corn from below and actually ravage the stacked sheaves and cause the Egyptians much trouble.

On that account the people try to trap them, to exclude them by building walls, to keep them oil by digging trenches in which they light fires. Now the Mice go nowhere near the traps but allow them to remain useless.

And al- though the walls have been rendered smooth with a wash of mortar, they climb up -them and then, being exceedingly nimble, jump over the trenches. And so the Egyptians abandon their traps and schemes as ineffectual and turn from them to prayers and supplications to the gods. Whereupon the Mice, I fancy, are in dread of the wrath of heaven and retreat in the formation of a hollow square to some mountain. Now the youngest go in front and the oldest bring up the rear, and if any are left behind, the latter turn and force them to follow.

If however the youngest ones halt from exhaustion, the entire lots behind them halt also, as is customary for an armed force. And when the front rank begins to move, then the remainder follows. And the inhabitants of Pontus say that the Mice there do the same.

And it is believed that whenever a house is threatening to fall, all the Mice will change house as fast as their legs can carry them. Now here is another peculiar trait of Mice: whenever they hear the squeak of a marten or the hiss of a viper they transfer their young from one hole to a number of different holes.

9. The story of crathis

An Italian story, which records an event that occurred when affairs were at their prime in the city of Sybaris, has reached me and is worth relating.

A mere boy, a goatherd by occupation, whose name was Crathis, under an erotic impulse lay with the prettiest of his goats, and took pleasure in the union, and whenever he wanted sexual pleasure he would go to her; and he kept her as his darling.

Moreover the amorous goatherd would bring to his loved one aforesaid such gifts as he could procure, offering her sometimes the loveliest twigs of tree-medick, and often bindweed and mastic to eat, so making her mouth fragrant for him if he should want to kiss her.

And he even prepared for her, as for a bride, a leafy bed ever so luxurious and soft to sleep in. But the he-goat, the leader of the flock, did not observe these proceedings with indifference, but was filled with jealousy.

For a time however he dissembled his anger and watched for the boy to be seated and asleep; and there he was, his face dropped forward on his chest. So with all the force at his command the he-goat dashed his head against him and smashed the fore-part of his skull.

The event reached the ears of the inhabitants, and it was no mean tomb that they erected for the boy; and they called their river 'the Crathis' after him. From his union with the she- goat a baby was born with the legs of a goat and the face of a man. The story goes that he was deified and was worshipped as a god of the woods and vales. From the goat we learn that animals have indeed their share of jealousy.

10. Ants and their nests

Historians celebrate the underground passages of the Egyptians; they also with the company of poets celebrate certain labyrinths in Crete. They have yet to learn of the elaborate tracks with their maze of windings dug by Ants in the earth.

Now in their wisdom these make their underground dwelling so very tortuous as to render access difficult or totally impossible for such creatures as have designs upon them. And the' soil which they excavate they put around the mouth, forming as it were walls and barriers, so that the rain which descends from the sky may not easily flood them and destroy all or at any rate most of them.

And with consummate skill they build partitioning walls, as you might say, to separate their cells from one another, and, as in some fine house, there will be three divisions: the first they design for the ' men's quarters,' in which the males live and any females that are with them; the second, in which the pregnant ants bring forth their young- the ' women's quarters,' as it might be; and the third they set apart as a treasury and a pit for the seeds they have collected.

And no Ischomachus, no Socrates, with their interest in the management of a household on admirable lines, is there to teach them these things. When Ants go abroad to collect food, they follow the biggest ones, and these lead the way, like generals.

And as soon as they reach the crops the young ones stand at the foot of the stalks while the leaders crawl up and having eaten through what are called the ' rhacillae ' of the fruitful ears, throw the ears down to the crowd below.

And these go about and cut off the chaff and peel off the capsules that protect and envelop the wheat. They need no threshing, no men who can winnow, nor even 'rushing winds' to separate and sunder the chaff and the grain, yet the Ants possess the food of men who plough and sow.

I have also heard the following example of their cleverness: their relations bury dead ants in the capsules of wheat, just as men bury their parents or all whom they love in coffins.

11. Birds and their enmities

The Francolin entertains the bitterest hatred for the Cock, and the Cock on its side for the Francolin; Likewise the Falcon for the Crow, and vice versa; and the Raven for the Sea-hawk and the Sea-hawk for it; the Raven and the Falcon for the Turtle-dove and the Turtle-dove for both.

I have learnt also that the Stork abhors the Bat, and the Bat in return abhors it as an enemy; and the Pelican, I am told, is not friendly disposed to the Quail, and their hatred is mutual.

Substances fatal to birds

To the Eagle the herb called comfrey is fatal; to the Ibis the gall of the Hyena; to the Starling the seed of garlic; to the Stone-curlew bitumen; to the Kite pondweed, as it is called. And the Kite cannot endure the gall of the Shearwater.

If a Falcon, or a Sea-mew, or a Turtledove, or a Black- bird, or the whole Vulture tribe eats a sliced pomegranate, they die. The leaves of the cedar are fatal to the Reed-warbler (?); the flower of the agnuscastus to the Marsh-tit; to the Raven the seed of the rocket. The Beetle is killed by perfume and the Hoopoe by the fat of a gazelle.

If a Crow comes upon the remains of flesh which a wolf has eaten, it is killed. A Lark is destroyed by mustard-seed and a Crane if it drinks the gum from a vine.

12. The Hare

It occurs to me at this point to speak of the Hare as follows. The Hare does not repair to its accustomed form until it has confused its tracks, here in entering, and there in leaving-, in order to defeat the designs of huntsmen. It is by some kind of natural sagacity that it tricks men so very craftily.

13. The Mare and its love for its foal

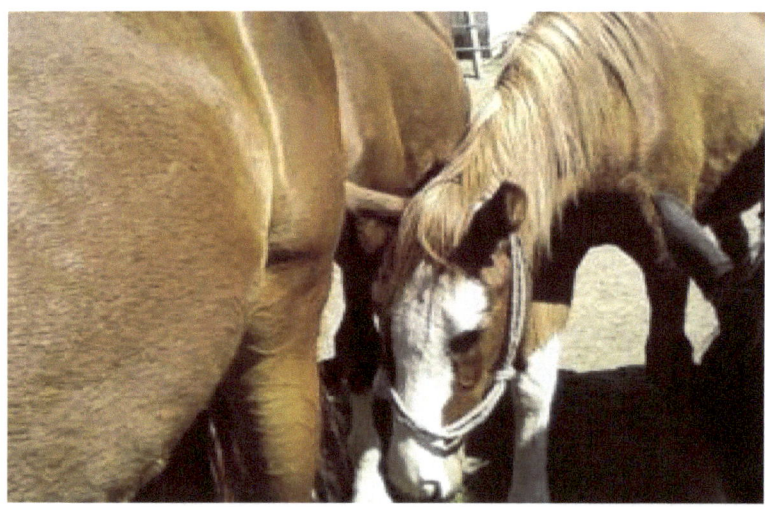

It seems that the Mare is in fact a good mother and cherishes the memory of her foal. The younger Darius had noted this; hence he would take into battle some mares that had lately foaled and had left their young at home.

Foals that lose their dams are reared on the milk of a stranger, just as human beings are. Now when the changing fortune of the battle of Issus began to press the Persians, and Darius was being defeated, he mounted a Mare, being anxious to escape and to save himself with all possible speed.

And the Mare, remembering the foal she had left behind, is celebrated for having with the uttermost eagerness and at full speed snatched her master away from the critical moment of urgent danger.

14. An aged Mule

At Athens an aged Mule was released from work by its master, so Aristotle tells us but declined to abandon its love of labour and its willingness to work on the score of age. Thus, at the time when the Athenians were erecting the Parthenon. Though it neither drew nor carried burdens, yet it would unbidden and of its own free will walk by the young mules as they went back and forth, like a horse harnessed alongside a pair, acting as guard, so to speak; and by treading a common path it encouraged their work, like some old craftsman whom age has released from labour with his hands but Whose experience and knowledge are a stimulus and incitement to the young.

Now when the people got to hear of this they directed the herald to proclaim that if it came in quest of barley meal or approached to get corn, it was not to be prevented but was to be allowed to eat its fill, and that the populace would defray the cost, as in the case of an athlete who in his old age was given his meals in the Prytaneum.

15. Cleanthes and the Ants

The following story, they say, shows how Cleanthes of Assos was forced against his will and in spite of his vehement arguments to the contrary, to make a concession to animals and to allow that they too are not destitute of reasoning power.

Cleanthes happened to be seated and moreover was resting quietly for some time. Now there were Ants about his feet in great numbers. So he observed how some were conveying a dead ant out of one track to a nest belonging to other ants not of their own kin.

And they paused on the edge of the nest with the corpse while others came up from below and met the strangers seemingly with a view to some consultation; the same Ants then went down into the nest.

And this happened several times until finally they brought up a worm, as it were a ransom. And the other party accepted it and surrendered the dead body which they had brought. And the Ants in the nest were glad to receive it, as though they were recovering a son or brother.

Now What answer can Hesiod make to this when he says that Zeus has made a distinction between various natures and has granted?' to fish on the one hand and to beasts and to Winged fowl that they should devour one another, for among them there is no justice, but to man-kind has he granted justice' ? But Priam will not admit this, since it was at the cost of many marvelous treasures that even he, a man and moreover a descendant of Zeus, redeemed Hector from the man who was also a hero and a descendant of Zeus.

16. The 'Dipsas' snake

The name of the Dips-as (thirst-provoker) declares to us what it does. It is smaller than the viper, but kills more swiftly, for persons who chance to be bitten burn with thirst and is on fire to drink and imbibe without stopping and in a little while burst.

Sostratus declares that the Dipsas is white, though it has two black stripes on its tail. And I have heard that some people call these snakes presteres (inflaters) ; others, kausones (burners). In fact they deluge this creature with a host of names.

It has also been called melanurus (black-tail), so they say, and by others ammobates (sand-crawler); and should you also hear it also called /centris (stinger), you may take it from me that the same snake is meant.

And it behooves me to repeat a story (which I know from having heard it) regarding this creature, so that I may not appear to be ignorant of it. It is said that Prometheus stole fire, and the story goes that Zeus was angered and bestowed upon those who laid information of the theft a drug to ward off old age. So they took it, as I am informed, and placed it upon an ass.

The ass proceeded with the load on its back; and it was summer time, and the ass came thirsting to a spring in its need for a drink. Now the snake which was guarding the spring tried to prevent it and force it back, and the ass in torment gave it as the price of the loving-cup the drug that it happened to be carrying.

And so there was an exchange of gifts: the ass got his drink and the snake sloughed his old age, receiving in addition, so the story goes, the ass's thirst.

What then? Did I invent the legend? I will deny it, for before me it is celebrated by Sophocles, the tragic poet, and Dinolochus, the rival of Epicharmus, and Ibycus of Rhegium, and the comic poets Aristias and Apollophanes.

17. An Elephant punishes dishonesty

Were I to pass over a piece of cleverness on the part of an Elephant, someone will say that I failed through ignorance to record it. And it is really worth hearing, so let us hear it.
The man who was entrusted with the care of its food was in the habit of purloining its corn, and by scattering stones underneath it he rendered most of the food uneatable, while preserving the bulk of the measure, so far as the master who supervised them both could see.
And for a while he escaped detection. So the Elephant, observing the designing fellow as he was cooking some porridge, picked up with its trunk a mass of sand at its feet and flung it into the pot, thus adroitly avenging the treatment it had received at his hands.

18. The Dog In Egypt

All other Dogs are clever at catching and tracking down wild animals; Egyptian Dogs however excel at running away. Thus, although they dread the creatures in the Nile, thirst compels them to drink, while their fear does not allow them to drink in peace as much as they want.

For that reason they do not put their heads down and drink, for fear some creature from below may creep up and seize them; and so they run along the brink, lapping with their tongue and snatching or, one might say, positively stealing their drink.

19. The Hedgehog

I have already mentioned many other crafty tricks of the Land Echinus (hedgehog), not the Sea Echinus (sea-urchin), but one specimen of its guile which I failed to mention I will mention now.

When it is likely to be caught it rolls itself up, which makes it impossible to handle; moreover it holds its breath and remains motionless and pretends to be dead.

20. The Limpet

You would not succeed in dislodging Limpets from the rocks, even were you to grasp them with the fingers of a Milo who clung with such strength and tenacity to a pomegranate tree that not one of his opponents could Wrench it from his right hand.

But anyone who undertakes to dislodge a Limpet from the rock to which it is clinging is laughed at for his pains and affords merriment to others. At all events it is impossible for him to get what he wants. An iron saw will at long last detach it from the rock.

21. The Elephant and its hunters

It appears that the Libyans do not confine themselves to waging war upon their neighbors with a view to gaining an advantage over them, but they wage War upon Elephants also. And the latter are well aware that the purpose of their attack is nothing else than to get their tusks.

So those beasts that have had one tusk mutilated stand in the front line, the rest of the herd using them as a cover in order that they may receive the first assault and that the rest may help with» the strength of their tusks un- damaged and equal to the struggle.

And perhaps they are trying to convince the Libyans and to prove to them that they are risking their lives for an inconsiderable reward. One of their tusks they use as a Weapon and keep sharpened; the other they use as a mattock, for with it they dig up roots and lever up and bend down trees.

22. The Spider's Web

It seems after all that Spiders are not only dexterous weavers after the manner of Athena the Worker and goddess of the Loom, but that they are by nature clever at geometry.

Thus, they keep to the centre and fix with the utmost precision the circle with its boundary based upon it, and have no need of Euclid, for they sit at the very middle and lie in wait for their prey.

And they are, as you might say, most excellent weavers and adept at repairing their web. And any thread that you may chance to break of their skilled and delicate workmanship they repair and render sound and whole again.

23. The Phoenix

The Phoenix knows how to reckon five hundred years without
the aid of arithmetic, for it is a pupil of all-wise Nature, so that
it has no need of fingers or anything else to aid it in the
understanding of numbers.

The purpose of this knowledge and the need for it are matters
of common report. But hardly a soul among the Egyptians
knows when the five- hundred-year period is completed; only
a very few know, and they belong to the priestly order.

But in fact the priests have difficulty in agreeing on these
points, and banter one another and maintain that it is not now
but at some date later than when it was due that the divine
bird will arrive. Meantime while they are vainly squabbling,
the bird miraculously guesses the period by signs and
appears.

And the priests are obliged to give way 6 and confess that they devote their time ' to putting the sun to rest with their talk ' but they do not know as much as birds. But, in G0d's name, is it not wise to know where Egypt is situated, where is Heliopolis whither the bird is destined to come, and where it must bury its father and in what kind of coffin?

But if there is nothing wonderful in all this, are we really to pronounce as ' wise ' affairs relating to the market, to armaments, and men's other schemes for their mutual undoing? I think not, you men who rival Sisyphus and the Cercopes and the Telchines.

I address myself to those who perfect themselves in these matters, but not to those who have not been initiated into the aforesaid abominations.

24. The dog, its reasoning power

If even animals know how to reason deductively, understand dialectic, and how to choose one thing in preference to another, we shall be justified in asserting that in all subjects Nature is an instructress without a rival.

For example, this was told me by one who had some experience in dialectic and was to some degree a devotee of the chase. There was a Hound, he said, trained to hunt; and so it was on the track of a hare.

And the hare was not yet to be seen, but the Hound pursuing came upon a ditch and was puzzled as to whether it had better follow to the left or to the right. And when it seemed to have weighed the matter sufficiently, it leapt straight across. So the man who professed himself both dialectician and huntsman essayed to offer the proof of his statements in the following manner: The Hound paused and reflected and said to itself: 'The hare turned either in this direction or in that or went ahead. It turned neither in this direction nor in that; therefore it went ahead.'

And in my opinion he was not being sophistical, for as no tracks were visible on the near side of the ditch, it remained that the hare must have jumped over the ditch. So the Hound was quite right also to jump over after it, for certainty that this particular Hound was good at tracking and keen-scented.

25. The Camel, its modesty

The Massagetae, according to Herodotus hang up their quivers in front of themselves and then the man has commerce with the woman openly, even though all can see, though in fact they pay no attention." Camels however would never couple in the open, nor if there were witnesses, so to say, looking on.

But whether we are to call this modesty or a mysterious gift of Nature, let us leave it to Democritus and others to decide and suppose themselves competent to investigate and explain the causes of matters obscure and past conjecture.

And even the herdsman at once takes himself off when he realises that the urge to couple is upon them, just as one withdraws when the bride and bridegroom are about to enter the marriage-chamber.

26. The Elephants respect for old age

Lycurgus laid down a most humane law (as I think), viz that younger men should give up their seats to, and leave the path for, their elders out of respect for years which all pray they may attain, if that chance to be their destiny.
But how could the noble son of Eunomus seek to rival and compete with the laws of Nature P At any rate, you lawgivers, men like Lycurgus," Solon, Zaleucus, and Charondas, the race of Elephants obeys laws which your legislation does not even begin to touch.

For all that, they behave in the following manner: the young ones give way to the elders in feeding; they wait upon those that are weak with age; they guard them from danger; when they fall into pits the young ones drag them out by throwing in armfuls, so to say, and bundles of dry sticks which the elders use as steps and so climb out, though burdened with age.

Where, I should like to know, did an Elephant ever belabor its sire with blows? Where, I ask, among Elephants did a sire ever disinherit its son P But perhaps, my fellow men, you who (if I am to speak the truth) fabricate and invent incredible tales, think that I am telling tales.

27. Gelon and his dog

What I have said above proves that the Dog certainly loves his master, and so I think I should put the following story beside the rest. Gelon of Syracuse while fast asleep fancied that he had been struck by Zeus.

But what he saw was only a dream; yet, although asleep he cried aloud and at the top of his voice. Whereupon a Dog which he kept, hearing the voice of its friend and comrade, as though Gelon's life was in danger from a plot, leapt with all its force on to the bed and stood over its master, barking furiously, as though it would keep off the assailant.

So Gelon was roused and through fear and the noise of barking threw off sleep though it was of the deepest.

28. Snake befriends boy

A young Snake was brought up along with a child, an
Arcadian born; the snake too was of the country. So as the pair
grew up the child became a youth while his foster-brother had
already become enormous.

And they were devoted to one another. But the relatives of the
youth were terrified at the size of the monster. (You may see
these creatures attain in a very short time to an enormous size
and the most terrifying aspect.) And so while it was asleep on
the same bed with the boy, they picked it up and took it as far
away as possible.

And the boy rose up, but the Snake remained in that place.
And when it took to the forest and the drugs that grew there,
it lived there, enjoying the food of snakes and preferring waste
places to life in a city and confinement in a room.

Time passed and turned one into a young man, the other into a Snake now full-grown. And on one occasion the Arcadian, the lover and the beloved of the aforesaid creature, going through a lonely region, fell in with brigands, and at a blow from a sword he cried out, as was natural, both from pain and in order to summon help.

Now it seems that the Snake of all creatures has the sharpest sight and the keenest hearing. Accordingly this Snake, being the youth's foster-brother, heard his voice and hissing loudly as in anger, struck terror into the brigands, who were seized with trembling: the villains were all scattered in different directions, and what is more, some were overtaken by the Snake and perished miserably.

But the Snake cleansed the wounds of its old friend, and after escorting him past that part of the region where wild beasts lurked, departed and Went to the spot Where the relations had exposed it : it showed no resentment at having been cast away, nor did it in the hour of danger, like base men, neglect one who had been its dearest friend.

Get All The Books In The Series:

Animal Peculiarity Volume 1 [1-8]
Animal Peculiarity Volume 2 [1-8]